DWELLING SONG

Dwelling Song

POEMS BY SALLY KEITH

The University of Georgia Press Athens and London

Bread Loaf 2019

For Peggy —
with fond memories &
hope for all our
future poems

xo Sally

Published by the University of Georgia Press
Athens, Georgia 30602
www.ugapress.org
© 2004 by Sally Keith
Designed by Mindy Basinger Hill
Set in 10.5/14 Filosofia

Printed digitally in the United States of America

Library of Congress Cataloging-in-Publication Data

Keith, Sally.
   Dwelling song : poems / by Sally Keith.
   68 p. ; 22 cm. — (The contemporary poetry series)
   ISBN 0-8203-2599-6 (pbk. : alk. paper)
   I. Title. II. Contemporary poetry series (University of
   Georgia Press)

PS3561.E3773D85 2004
811'.6—dc22

                                        2003022004
   ISBN-13: 978-0-8203-2599-6

British Library Cataloging-in-Publication Data available

Grateful acknowledgment is made to the editors of the follow-
ing publications, in which some of these poems first appeared:
*American Letters and Commentary, Born Magazine, Colorado Review,
Conjunctions, CUE, Denver Quarterly, Facture, Interim, Literary Imagi-
nation, New England Review, No: A Journal of the Arts, Phoebe, Slope,
Web Conjunctions, West Branch,* and *Common Wealth: Contemporary
Poets of Virginia* (The University of Virginia Press).

I have built thee an exalted house,

a place for thee to dwell in forever.

2 CHRONICLES 6:2

CONTENTS

The Gallery   3

The Hunters   7
Song from the Riverbed   9
Orphean Song   11
Relocation   13
Song from the Street   18
Declensions   19
Bottle-Notes   21
Subtraction Song   24

Rooms Where We Are   29

Elegy   47
Song from the Ridge   49
Restoration   52
Song from the Frozen Field   53
Tessellation   55
A Heretic Song   57
Self-Portrait after the Snow   60
Song from the Rain   62

Beacon Line   67

I'm sitting in the kitchen and
  I've thought to list the things
that line the little town
    in me. I've thought to hang
my portraits on these walls, where
    light is stretching, already, though
it seems, at three, too soon. One,
    a door ajar. But the strokes are too thick
and if inside it's night, some lighter hue is
    leaking in. In Two
you left and the fog fell. Didn't I write
    to tell you? This painting is gray. There were shapes
underneath. I can't read them,
    now. It doesn't rise. Wet and it doesn't rise.
I'm taking notes on this envelope because
    the concerto adds to a slowness
in the leaves, blown off, see, and digging
    shallow trenches in the snow.
Three, where no color was
    the willow wisps to yellow were
stripped, and the willow in front of
    the grander, brownish-black trees. Underneath
a pail. In it stones. I picked one up
    and still damp from the snow
it shone.
    I write: it is currently seven degrees. In this
gentle after-breeze the body of
    the trenched leaf mechanically blows
open, falls closed like a lid. Four,
    the footprints in the frozen snow, false
tacks. I write it: Who is this cozening
    hidden lord who leads me? Five,
a drowning and a line.

It is I. And you must
never cross nor ever trust beyond it.
    My legs are hidden and kicking. Salt
still burns in my lungs. The concerto then
    was not to be played and we didn't want
that portrait to be seen. Six, then,
        is in the form of a dream
where the earth went white and into the sky
    a magnificent fiery red. It is seeing what
I'm not supposed to see. Inside the closet, if I open
        the door, a pool of burning light.
Seven, it may have been the ocean
    an infinitude of wave-framed plates that catch
each bit of sun from the day, unfailingly. So caught
        it's carried, collided. This is where I can't
believe. It must have been a prayer. Eight, it could have been
        the field covered in snow, but broken by
the stalks—a metal collage where
        the can's sharp edge folds
against a bar of heavier lead. Where the edge juts.
    Where we should not touch. We should not—
Nine, you know this. Here nothing crept.
    The violinist plays exactly how
she meant to play. We keep pushing. But
    light roils until it is thin and then
it goes away. We should not—
    You know this. The door shuts.
And in Ten it shuts so it slams.

THE HUNTERS

Their return didn't flutter, what body it had
   it tamped—it moved in slow progression
their legs leaving hollowed dents

   in snow; the dogs, behind them, hanging
their heads, then, further—something between
   desperation and attempt. Here

the knot on the nerve in my neck *mark me—*
   my armor incomplete
the dark color shuffling, thicker

   than cards and thicker than rope, and
the quicker the speed the harder
   my hope. The hunters (call them: knights, call

their armor: burlap sacks, call their swords: wooden
   shafts) have almost cleared the wood. Count
the few bare elm. They dodge them, according to

   gravitational chance. The rods go down
with the slant of the hill and the hurry of dogs
   sounds on their heels—they keep it at their backs.

Walk in these woods. Leave that. I'd pull down
   my woolen cap, cinch my tired eyes
to my feet. What can they wear, that would let me—

   when I am handed over? What will I speak?
Can the village know? Couched in hills it holds
   a solemn hum against the thicker

blacker beat. And the cottages line the rectangular
    lake. And the lake is frozen. And the children,
unaware of their pattern, gleefully skate. The wind

    is the only resistance they know. *Mark me.*
Death is the pebble, is slipped from the bridge
    as we finish descending the hill, slipped

by the unknown foot. Listen. It hits. *Leave
    that.* Listen. The children are shrieking.
Shall not. Shall not. Pull down my woolen cap.

    Now, Sunday morning, we return. No
children. The steeple inextricable—the given
    in a village shape. We look to it. Tomorrow and—

Mercy. Mercy. Death is—
    The ghost. The choir. The almost sound
rising up. Belt, breastplate, helmet, my sword

    of—this skin beats too fast. *Walk in
these woods.* There were three birds, wings touching
    contented. I am returning. I'll sit

by the fire with my only wife. I'll go
    for bread by dawn and wood by dusk.
I'll study the bird that is left, cutting

    winter's only sky. Lonely,
or, at last. *Mercy. Mark me.* To hold it—
    feathered and nothing—I'd try.

SONG FROM THE RIVERBED

As mica gleamed and salt-sized grains caught noon light
and lifted off what silken seemed, a sheet, a case
but thin, but bright

a gale touched down, through what and when
I know not—no haze would stick, so shelter like
a shadow stretched

hung from where the bank bent
back. Yes, still life:

it shed cool black. Yes,
blank shelf: what wants will

hallow what lives without. Watch how fast
in sun the drops on yet pale skin still lift.

See how dim white rings the stones with water marks.
What other world is thus dug out?
River-weight,

lead-line, rocks for where the bank slipped
back. Here, I wash the silt from one.
I hold it in my hand.

Leaving-myth:
I read all my clues.

The rocks went tumbling down.
Then. this broke the rule—

Spring came,

the river blued, began in sequined discs to shine
and purple lined the steps they've dug into the banks in town.
Around me, new birds

swooped down. Around me, darting bird bodies
opened to shuffle midday's flat light.
Wing-math, I accept.

So from the length of the blur, we gathered the speed.
So from the speed of the river, we figured how fast they flew.

But something is waving.
On the horizon, some backless thing staggers

and flags and stubbornly, say leadenly, it is repeating itself
refusing and refusing to rise.

ORPHEAN SONG

Dear smoke: It puzzles

    and it shuts me in my room where I dream
of home—a folder full of flowers, not pressed.
Your photograph, I've caved it
for the keeping jar and I'm afraid: I've bent
the brow, the hair not meant to move again.

Dear you: Confess

    How many ways am I missing?
I've lost our final folding doll, so stole
a splash of night to hold it in this vacant pear.
I fear the viceroy wing I've framed
tacked in glass, hung where I stare on the pane.

        The sky keeps coming.
And if color will, I am, but if the wing is split
again, I'm wrong—the filaments will splinter
and yellow open so glints go glitter and this
I'll brush away—deceived before.

Dear law: I got caught

    I was singing when they spied me.
The peasants got scared and dropped their forks
leaving the fallow fields, leaving
light stuck on the metal and the sound
of that song got stopped there in the stones.

The details do not improve.
Me muscle, me skin, and me bones,
but once a land and it grew. The wind turned white,
the undersides of leaves, they bled with the sun
on the tops of the others and here is the sound—

Dear one: Name this

    a stair dug for the day, a song
so it beckons and it pulls me through
the holes in the leaves. They've found me
glancing through to the base of the mound.
I found swarthy-like torches of red.

        I was willing then to sing again.
I'm out for my walk on the line.
When I reach the top of the road
the blackness lifts. It turns and in turning
it's swelling to two large clouds—

Dear love: A ladder

    in between. One falling to
the other. One drops
a flight of stairs. These are bones
in the sky. Fossils. A broken
cage. Washboard prayer.

        A missing tongue, pressing
its only word. Sad and
stammering on—Dear dear:
free, I'm free,
free, I'm asking

RELOCATION

1.

Arrived, a day.
            I have tried to say:
there is a man who steps from his porch in the plains
steps into widening streaks of whitening light
steps into slight—
            I have tried to understand,
not this walking out into a field. I would walk forever out into—

I have contemplated and I have studied
his return. Is he a runnel there? Do the windrows act
as a track, the inevitable? Do they only point him back?

He is not avoiding the mounds that are airy
loose and given to collapse.

His shoes are old sneakers.
Each morning he feels this—a falling

as the soles flex with each step
and press into the arcs of his feet.

2.

Arrived, a day.
        The commotion at the café begins:
Bad Dog Sit,
        as the small terrier pulls from the table where he is tied
and the boy, of the woman who owns it, straddles it, clasps
his short arms around the dog's lurching neck.

This scene repeats itself like a wave.

The sun is setting.
        Bad Dog Sit.

Four boxwoods in a mulch bed throw irregular-shaped shadows.

Distracted, I study precision.

As the sun sinks farther the black shapes stretch to single lines
and where a branch may jut, a patch of lightness intrudes.

Then in the blackness there must be small hooks.
Shadow-weave and untouchable net: it must connect.

        Bad Dog Sit.

And the chair beside me pushes back.
And finally they untie it and gather their belongings.

Now they leave.

3.

Arrived, a day.

Arrived, a day, interrupted.

Do this. Sip coffee. Remember to photocopy.

Remember the fog from the summer—

not continuous, a press of fog, a shard thrown out
over the field and stuck as if parsing, making a rim,
parsing, unpredictable, red, an instance of memory

now distant. Do this. Sip coffee. Remember—

Looking down, I am tired of the trees outside my window
without pattern. I'm studying precision.
Their gold color fading.

I am tired of these roofs,
without system. Stop wondering. Sip coffee.

Roll the blinds to aim the light upward.
Remember. I am afraid of—

without you—
some slow moving backwards.

4.

Arrived, a day.

To write the world outward, two years past and still leaves
                                        turning in—
            siphoned of color, variety of vein determining the life of leaf
                                                        on the tree.

To write to lost gold, to the red rim that fell, to throw words—
                        I am small throwing words
            studying precision.

To write, two years past, I'm still stuck in the layers of things.

Two years past and I lie—

                        what I face I have no answer to.

A house, a neighborhood, two rivers, and—

Distracted, I study—

But as the wind beats the river
            as a line of water is driven by wind, as the wind
            angles downward and slaps the water to squares
            so that the greater the force, the farther the waves
            rise from the flat—
                        the river leads.

My voice is driven hard against me.

One on my left and one on my right,
I'm threaded here with rivers for the corners of my eyes.

And when I went where the rivers joined the bay
and entered the ocean, so to cure me—

I could not study anymore.
On a point there was a width.

I found it ghostly. I found it gray.

This is a cat running. This is the fur running across the ribs, running across the street. These are the mules. I call them mules. They pull a cart, heads bashing against the wall, noses (I mean) kissing the side of a bar. Back. Drinking. Pointing. Pointing at their mules (forward and back) running up against the wall. This is the shop window and how it looks when it is dark. Now the espresso maker that no one will buy. These are concrete telephone posts. I mean they also hoist lights and then lines run across the street. I mean not everyone has a telephone. This is her mouth cutting the dark saying it isn't because I want to be nice (now). Here is the truth smacked up against stillness. This is the khaki rain, no this is the khaki jacket pulled tight across her chest. This is the front door of the school, the street I've called long and narrow, the time when we are supposed to let vision have permanence. No, this is the time when vision becomes a fragment of what we remember and the repetitions sing themselves away again. That was her face lost in the shadow of a tree and the white space moving in and out. Those were four legs made shadows on the lower half of a green wall. This is repetition. This is walking down the street. Now I have emotion with shoes on. Now I believe myself even with shoes on. I mean I understand what is happening. This is the evidence. You can unlock a door in the dark.

DECLENSIONS

In countable pieces of choppy flight
   a summer hummingbird returns.
The equation keeps balancing out, and
   I'm drawn to how it does not settle—

the bobber as the fish strikes, the black magnet
   clapping black, the charm. Maybe
we spring and clutch from wired lines, and maybe
   we hang awry. Here is the moment,

middle of winter, everything dead, when particles
   soften and what, first, felt brittle goes
round—the season will end. Think of the train
   threading the land, the branches as half

the lesson. Here, the man soldiers too far
   into the street, head down,
bag in each hand, and the truck is moving too slow
   because of him. I'm putting back

the pieces, hanging the journey, country to city,
   arranging the palettes on the line.
In the middle, quarter way from home—
   a shepherd. The color around him, his sheep.

The train goes faster. He and his sheep are a shape
   hovering and symbiotic with the hill.
I'm here to report the mimicries I've found:
   the clothesline curve, gone polyhedral

holding the heavy squares; the dried twig
   leaves along the river, hundreds
of paper hands in prayer or loss, rolled up
   or reaching out; the river, itself, freezing

unfreezing in a misshapen line—the line reflecting
　　the flight of the birds, pale-gray
on strong white, pausing at the apex
　　of each curve, like taking in air, like air

the thing they need. And now the shepherd goes home.
　　It is night. And he washes his hands
before sleep. *I will live in a room with the things*
　　I need and I haven't decided

how I'll get out. The hills surrounding look stark
　　as the last shadows darken and stretch
and the lake in the distance keeps catching
　　old light from the moon.

BOTTLE-NOTES

I took where summer stopped
and fields to river fell and halved
the width and windrow halved

to mark my center: this. I took
the seventh glass, to tell
me how to store—to drop inside

of one where trumpet blew
a berry's thickening red past black.
I—guessed then plucked,

from single fruit, the wispy thorn
attached. And half of me
cannot confess. In crystalline—

a clod-size knot found caught
in scaly oyster dust and stone.
Be stone or pebble, be

the life in death into—the—be
obsidian, be jeweled
sound, be dropped in harrowed glass

be caught by almond white
where centers stacked—a petal bed
I made the middles, and

to this I called: collapse.
And half of me cannot
pray. Wiry veins press

on glass. But, straighter, still
the knobbed twig grid, nest-
swatch. My veil—

my almost black. In this
space stands taut. Sworn
to. It will. A prayer to

addition. Then a hollow
wing rod, because the steeple
would not fit. So, flight—

the glass contains and marks
the plea, here, alight—
but broke. And then to what

to cling? I sought a straight
line. And what believed
I said, float. Or—hide? Rod,

rake tine, or twig? I knew
how not to look. And
covered them up. But—

I'd left out light.
Could not keep
it in. What chose

to unrest me—I don't
know. Here, for you, I
wrote a note: *please.*

SUBTRACTION SONG

My real name got lost in the letter
I kept trying to write. There I was.

I'd sketched the field with Queen Anne's lace
the radial heads I'd given in
mathematical light. Two then:

I use a ruler to extend the planes.
Pullied and chained, they intersect.
They build me this crosshatched house.

I had an addressee.
I have a tangled house.
Two then: I'm making this object

and it equals a song. And the song's to be sung
in the church. And the roof of the church is to house
the song. And the house is what we'll offer up.

One: are you leaving?

> (Two then: I reread my museum note:
> *Skeleton-cage, what is empty?*)

The object, here, a handmade wooden box.
Extend the planes. Examine the arrows.
Study the torque.

Is light in there? It matters.
It matters like the candle's steel flames
still brief, the soft sound

dominoes make falling in a line
if the floor is made of wood.

Two then: don't speak for now.
And One is off to sleep.
Two then: are they stuck inside you?

I answered: stone ghosts.
I answered: congealing.
        (Two then: then fly away, fly away all.)
I answered: thick throat.

        (One: I reread my note from June:
                A man and a woman stand in a clearing
                their shadows drop in the hands of a clock.
                Their shadows stop and the couple slips
                into the circling trees.)

Two then: stop flying.
And One.
Two then: help me through

the fact of you.
And One whispers:
open the box.

        (Two then: I reread my note from May:
                Where gnats hurry in patches of slow pond air
                the world shuts—a quaking lid. Consider this fact:
                I'm sitting here. Here things don't leave.)

And I didn't know then. I'd called the stone
my final proof, sunk in the center of the field,
sunk at the foot of the tree. And there I'd leaned

singing you the song as you sat
in your box, singing once the shadows
lifted off and went away—

The elegy sang itself blue for the rock.
Two then: I've studied how we're meant to act.
And One. He cried himself to sleep.

>   (In my notes the sand crabs were dusty white
>   the white of no reflection, the white in which
>   things sink. And by moonlight, the crabs
>   slipped from the sand to the sea.)

Two then:
Love-veil, what color are you?
One, in silence, went white.

>   (Two then: I reread my notes to find fragments of letters:
>   *Dear One—Today is.*
>   *And the sun for the first time in weeks.)*

Two then: if you can pry the planks
call my name. Apprentice me there.
There in the chance of that light.

One calls:

>   (Two: I reread my notes that label the box:
>   *A carpet rolled up.*
>   *An ocean pulled out. Tangles and chokes.*
>   *All pulling. Frays at the edge.*
>   *The sound you make falling after me.*
>   *That crashing sound the fact makes.)*

Two then:

One.

If turquoise goes on
autumn's gold   and flag
flagged down blew through.
If parallel   un-math this

code and you.   If
lied and if   lied
one unwraps another   and
              who is the keeper

of you?   I sent
it   if glass   if
water makes glass   if
flags make water and

fly.   I said it.
I saw one kissing
you   and I shall
eat grass and   die.

What   rote cry   croaked
into   my   rocking   room
woke me—   wrecked?
The mirror broke   spilled

dehisced. Reflection is—
plank   afloat   my   bed
on a boat   white
walls   this face stoned

by time   a nothingness
floating up   a grain
sifting down. What blocks
  a mirror's glass sight?

I can't see through.
    Nor parse   nor thread.
Let in.   Look past.
I heard and rose.

When waking was screaming
the line shot forth.
        It was not warped.
I had no idea

and wanted   one.   And
wanted.   I counted   false
anniversariessticks jammed into
a broom.   The walls

were watery   words not
parsed. Melting partita   I
bade the   coming   chord
home   again   alone.   Grid

without origin tangents collapsing
we're spinning   O accordion
oak-leaved table   books fading
the paperwhites protest—

Light where I left
        the sheets a knot
slips the bed   spans
the trim between floor

and wall   so splits
to stain   the grain
an amber gold   so
empty stands my wall.

Snapshot   the pale tin
            pot upon the table.
It's interrupting me   this
loose-hinged light turning

my room   this flitting
as dust falls from
the curving amaryllis anthers
            that will not finish.

Farther into the center
I broke   I dug
to find what shifting
sound   had reeled me

here. And nothing was.
No voice.   No box.
Lied. And lied   again.
So took myself in

for punishing.   No judge
was there   to hear.
Begging then began—
          To what should this

body sentenced turn? Then
the ghosting sounds   again.
Lurk.   Define smokelike—
Tell   where you are

Where shadow wefts weave
coercive convincing noon quits
                noon's quick mark—
stopgap—   it held

so that forward going
froze the trellised shadow's
pulling back.   How bright
the day is

burning dustless shot through
water glass   half rainbow
                quavering so—
sustenance stops. Day's clench

is culled forward but
                leaning back
and riven and wrestling
                with—

I caverned   I caved
to the corridor's light
partial and mazy. Distant
now the train cry

in the eye in
the floorboard's   dark ring
                    the skein of it
one moment after oncoming

train.   The sound must
come. Here   dark core
        I did know noon.
In light beams cut

life flies   cut moth
wings like leaves catch
floating light.   We are
near   and then—

The room where I'm
kept is all   glass.
The map   I   inhabit
thin   my walls I

coat in dust   from
shells   that I've razed
myself.   The nacre wearies
me.   I lack attention

too often turn to
the river below.   I
       hope it will light
blue and shine brazen

brash attention seeking send
message scrawling. For this
I clear a wall.
                    I keep a math.

Something inside this house
won't hum.   The sound
of waves is gone
         the weight of them

thrown down   dragged back
still some rasping   sound
slips   a gathering in
thin groves of bare

trees   holding the heavy
hurl of wind   from
my house   thin walls.
I wonder what will

break me?   Why won't
it come in   this
wind so invisible   still
lingering still lulling me.

But light is not

              wind. I sent it.

And the sky went

gray   lost texture. I

tried to still it.

        Then smoke. Then cars.

Then diagonally.   A gull

cutting across then screaming.

Let me live—
           where cove ice is
coming fast   where gulls
cinch invisible lines rise

on updrafts.   What grace
is that?   To drop
shelled sustenance   lower to
feast?   My dream was

me   a boat again
a middle and—
           all night the ice
got thick surrounding me.

I stayed.   Wind harried
it hard   shaking it
into and then   against
the shape of   itself.

I did not leave.
Inside   it lights by
lamp unevenly. In false
light then   I sit

considering the gloaming of
an eve   an elsewhere
            chance of red light
red fruit in wooden

bowls   now ripening   green
            moss on cottage walls
purple crocuses breaking spring's
black earth   a hand

breaking for example a
breeze of no color
my hand moving   then
   across your silent face.

                    Then   one half-chime
fell   broke but light
recombinant   airy   heard calling
from stagnant pools   thought

rending what   I want
the part in you that I heard hum
nerved thing   calling corners
from wall   what was it thought it

        would   calling dust up
into dawn   into pale
half-gold   thought would hold
this room   place light

dulling paint   yellow sheaves
would hold   reed curling
this calling   otherwise shaken
this room so empty

Inside   a memory broke
the silver lake   spreading
a stage   between riotous
delves of rock-lined earth

where we last August
sat our thinking   then
a dash   between poles
like splitting the night

and night a dome
black brushed by moonlit
streaks of cloud   water
    whipped by silver light

was edging the   waves
and the whistles   were
the throaty cries   of
night birds nesting afar.

I killed the empty
room. I broke the
bulb and bent the
chord. It looks the

same. Broke and killed.
It looks the same.
        Bodied and blue.
I didn't see

you.   And field and.
I killed the empty
room. And field and.
It looks the same.

Here I am waiting.
I haven't seen you.
I'm in these blades
of light. And field.

Tiny stalks.　Broken frames.
Corners of.　　Stick brooms.
T-squares bent.　　On end.
Side by side. I.

Angled greater-thans. Sky admitting.
What speaks?　　　　Pedicels by
peduncle.　There.　Gulls cry.
Sun streaks.　　　So violently.

Adornment then. Transient thing.
Frail gate.　　　　Gate for.
Frail cell.　Imagine in.
Bright bay.　　　Slight pink.

Beautiful scene.　Imagine. I.
I have feared coming.
Saddened by not.　　Now
night heaves.　Speaking of.

ELEGY

If how the buzzard blots the sky explains
    why half our kitchen lily fell,
then here the river cords the belt, tightly
    it threads the screw; in picking up

it moves. Upstairs the woman writes a letter.
    Know this: the cardigan falls
off the back of her chair. Stilled life,
    I've decided nothing, found no pattern

for light on snow in morning, no rule
    for the stutter-time a wing requires.
These days are like shipyards, mechanical and gray
    where sometimes water casting the street

catches an angle, oblique, of the sun, and pulls
    the day to sheen. Could you see? Yes—
so heavy the freighters arrive and depart,
    so mindlessly the waves

ascend the concrete bank, to slip, black
    and thin. Each lap, each subject, verb,
and object she writes, each dawn the sun's chance
    of lighting the fence in the neighbor's yard

and it differs daily by plank. Each print word,
    wet stone, square month, each asks:
will the weapon ever flower, will the lapsed
    thing rise, will I know the piece to return?

Consider, first, the city bird feather
    framed on the sidewalk after a morning rain,
the gray descending into white, the hollow divisor
    unevenly dividing, soldering

thirds, here two against one, and the strands
    of feather, silk gone coarse, that had been blown
in flight, turn back at random intervals.
    Turn back. Where the frozen river folds

the buzzard, one, like crucified, arm-wings
    automatic in stretch. Turn
back. Where needled light had passed the base
    of the tree and gathered in shallow puddles,

the sun's blush daubs are gold-shot
    rays. Between me and the particles
speckling the snow in silver, the distance increases
    and the further the wildflowers lean from the house

in truth, the further they die. Did you even
    make a sound? Because this death
convinces me: there is an ocean
    far away. It is not held in ice.

There is no map for how the sand turns
    black in lines to mark the waves'
hypnotic swelling, keeping each edge,
    for us, uncertain. See: she is stopping

the words at the margin. See: the house shuts
    between the buzzard's weighty wings.
The air around us could have been summer,
    see: it even sang.

SONG FROM THE RIDGE

A blue-gray opacity blots
   most of afternoon sky.
This storm has yet to arrive.
   In what is not yet thick.

pulled clouds like a swatch
   of thinning sheet, like an experiment
postering the sky, pressed
   between slide and coverslip

so that the edges
   the cloud parts pushing out
are luminescence, bright
   white letting small glint

but not for experiment
   only. *The storm has yet to arrive*
one cries, almost holding
   the other and certain

she will fall.
   The catching thing is not
aligned. As paper burns
   in the gullies, running

alongside the rail—
   I am the passenger.
I'm looking out
   when something cries—

It is the fire line, determined
    to enter (even determined
to leave) the city. *There is some place*
    or someone says the blood

in the spawning salmon's fast run
    say the bodies in a boat, traveling
down, lowered by locks,
    says the grit inside the words

like a bead on a string, privy
    to dips, even to small pieces
of wind. As if distinction
    were something

and something could make
    a mark, the hawk in the dead tree
repeats descent, because
    the smallest thing began

to shift, or motion
    the bird insists; maybe
invisible tracks traverse
    the field and the next station

is better than this. The body
    turns in pattern to flight
as unconcerned as the slabs
    of orange light, now

entering. Heaviness leaves
    the scene like paper wings
like something blown
    from its core and then

the beating wisps. Like I
   left me here and momentum
has cleared a path
   where the risen thing

is running to, even
   alone, with nothing else.
And at last the sky
   goes light before dusk.

The line is neck centered, halving the body's weight so that her stance has no jut. It has no awkward lean. Her hands fit inside of her face, like fretting, a wall, relief. These hands that throw the axe and plumb the earth—furiously they nail the beams together. They split the cloth to wrap a wound. They nimbly thread the eye to fix a gown. They fit—almost beautiful, struck, wheezing, and gray. They make a cave for the eyes, but light still slips in finger slats, unevenly, giving night a yellow-blue. But behind her hands, imagine, her eyes staying shut—the bolt for a twice-chained door.

Stay. The picket fence, even if storm blown, I'll come to do the painting, I'll come to tear the forsythia away. The bluebird house, even if the jays. I'll come. I'll stand in the field with you. See, already, I'm scaring them away. I'm waving my arms, mad, in the sky. Then the old farmhouse, because I've studied the order they fall. The window frames go out from their squares. The façade like a hand of splayed cards. The roof begins to buckle. Then the people leave. A chair gets left on the porch. Splotches of copper decay on the legs. And then begins the floor. Stay. I'll bring in a lamp and light us a corner. I'll bring in a plant and two chairs. We will live.

Light is pouring through the dust, breeding in beams, making a fugue for dark walls. I want to sit with you. Come back from the fields. Look, I'm stopped in the space of this door. It is calm here. Even if the wind is blowing, lifting the siding up from the house, swirling the dirt to eddies and branding a silvery sheen on the soy. Even if you think you can't forget the storm. Look, now. Ignore the wind. Ignore the watery, watery road.

SONG FROM THE FROZEN FIELD

Here is the gown
lashing to tear the frozen ground
drawing up dusty lines, but snow

a track to hold the wind
as it rolls, the cords so I know
the sky won't alight, the veins

webbing one and one to the other
and the wind won't stop anymore.
Limitless eve, part of me fades.

With strong resolve, the sun
is sinking so that red tinge razes
where what I'd named oblivion just left.

The cloud's gray skeins stretch
at farthest edge, thin and blurred,
as if a rigging might work—

the slate-colored ramp, hollowed out,
leaving an arrowlike roof, digs
a corner for the globe. Forcibly tonight

the pull. One wants to go.
Murderous haunt of white on white
lead me through this world afloat.

I know the field has melted once
and how repeatedly it froze.
Puddles now swell. The odd

collection can only increase: pools
go isles, between them thick snow
drifts, chiseled to imbricate gills

chiseled to wings. Still flight
has fallen more than once,
I know. I believe the field

is worlded with ships, sails all backing
the blades of wind, masts whirling
the whitening plane as disparate staves.

And one sinks. Another one knows:
the ocean isn't pierced by bells
isn't tinny, isn't bright.

No larkspur. No paintbrush.
Even in the dead of night, if dreaming
could descend the ice, find fuchsia

petals balled tight, find
white breaks and as it breaks
one throws down this finest net

and empty and burning it only returns.
Unfair night, where is the part that left?
Where is the killing, where the dream?

Middle world, no. Not yet.

Somewhere one's rising to find the other,
to gather the dust to piece back together
his throat.

Dear ghost, know this:
it is not you I stay away from
in this field of white.

TESSELLATION

When door on whisper opens fast
the sun-hat on parapet is blown

swiftly gone; two black-winged birds
in tangle rise a knot, a gumming

squall (the unsuspected heart
escapes the yellow field of hay)

to catch the thing that moves, unwrap
and scout; the moment for kites, distanced

by wind, breaking the law: one
in one will go. Or: fall from. Inside

the black lock's inky pool, the notch
it sticks and glues. It shuts the door

to keep the whisper out. Call this:
the upstairs room. But steps dissolve

to plane, a floor, and upward the flock
begins to rise. I—thumbish

the newel and squalling amongst
their fast debris, touched and touching

nothing. I want to catch one, wrap
the bird with wire, in binding hope.

I'll find one—to stay. One rock in river-
bed or warped pier plank, with

black-rust nails inside—one keeping
like the shore's inscrutable slant

to the sea. The hat now turned on side
pushed and pulled in step-shaped gusts

is pushing, but tangles at vortices
until wind will catch and then it begins,

it lifts, escaping the line it trailed
and fast turns flat, sailing the air

scouting imagined slides to let
it drop. It hopes to reach

the waves, where flat it falls, the brim
beginning, from water, to warp, to stick

and glue. In shutting this door it steeps
the hem, the inscrutable slant to the sea.

A HERETIC SONG

No, not here again, them telling "You're in, You're in."
I'm not. It's noon. I'm stopped
by my spot on the stoop.

I measure out the height of me to mark
my distance from the door. Lay my body
down if you don't believe—

how else can you keep yourself apart? If come upon
the stream on a blue day when because of
the rocks breaking

the surface, occasionally, and cleaving water's
downward flight so that the sun
strikes down in swords

of pinning, pinning light. Help me. How close
can I get? Tomorrow—Sunday.
Doors open, people flood.

I often retreat to the tops of the hills.
The problem persists: I take time
to see: junkyard boat

in the gully and dust on the aster from the road
then telephone poles, on one side
awkward forks—outward leaning

hinting me. The road hinting, trying
to evenly cut the field. But packed the land
beneath succeeds.

At dusk, I'm standing three-quarters up
the hill to watch a fire blaze.
The bean fields are yellow

and red and framed by green and the green
gives purple so that the orange
is lined with a near-

black haze. No, never inward
can I get. I've seen paintings of it.
I've reached the top.

But if you've heard the thunder bowling
around this thing by night, you know
we're caught.

On desperate days I've laid one arm
on top of the other. It helps.
I've emptied out

my head. And this is all I got—
night song—
wordless throat

and roving hum that culls the patches
of black. And am I wrong reknitting
me? Me miscreant.

What ever did I do? Miscue?
Miscue? The mise-en-scène off balance
(just as I've lifted

my camera to catch). Miser. I am
a mite dismayed. Mizzen shrouds,
auger holes, each

superfluous mast. Yes, I would sail
away. Finally, I would go. Look:
now the wind just beginning

to blow, as paint chips off the blue
buckling hull. Note: shatters of,
glints of, and all

in the gully. See me gathering
chalky shards, the arrows of color.
Blue jar. Thick

light. Why are we everywhere? Why
hanging? Why hung? And so if trophies
whose is this cloudy night?

SELF-PORTRAIT AFTER THE SNOW

And then the ground got soaked. Something
said: a skeleton in midnight, it will
sing. Blue was

blue are, blue: show me the
world's new crèche. The blown. We are
coming. We have come to

winter for. We then left. And then and then
Queen Anne's lace it left;
gone. Went to the wire of the

lady of my latter life, her
rolling hair, her pink and porcelain
face, the pinafore

stitch, the petticoat, the bowling out from her
little liney waist. So why
won't I soak?

Something said: note the pendentives
float the dome on top. And I: so
slide me to the square. Let me to the

dance. The lacy one, the
hung from white. For who has got the strength of
leg to move the

cold of cloth? Something said: now where it
hems it doubles, where it doubles it
slides the floor. Where it

splits. Where it times. I have a tendency to
roam. And I said: yes, to
wrap my peregrine

bone with rope that I might stay. That I
might have—Said:
no. I am the city boy

bugling, corner-standing
blowing the walls of my sky-
scrapers straight. And what is it in my

throat? The thing. Peremptory. It
builds my own with—proof: am not, am is,
proof: spring comes. look:

rabbits shoot from beams of
truck-lamp light. It says: in-
side me nothing but

clouds. I'm rolled. Lie to me.
Lie. *Lie.* Because if it
covers me, I'll—

SONG FROM THE RAIN

Outside I hear the steady rain in tiers
   first on the tin roof, hitting
like on a buckskin snare, then
   it drips, both high and crisp
and from here this sounds like a hive.
   The cars streak by blurring it all.
The yellow bus looks midnight blue.
   The sound of the rain is a knocking—
relentless and gravity—
   like something I can't undo.
Inside the body
   the sound is full of mechanics
and pipes and screws. It arrives
   early in morning as two lamps
reflect in my dark windowpane.
   One lake map (the shape
of something horrible, ragged
   in flight and impossible, with ripped
wings) so small in its frame
   and the sound of the rain is crossing
that lake in my mind, in a boat
   in heavy wind and in rain.
Inside the sound and suddenly
   I notice what wanting may be.
I ask what complexity is—
   I ask what is joy—
and smaller drips hit what sounds like a stream
   fast moving, out from a gutter.
It's nothing that floats; it's rusting
   blades on a fan; dumpsters
of stones inside construction sites;
   a restauranteur's new shipment of spoons.
The day before me is this rain,
   this game of darts where we throw

for speed, we throw for force and
    to win. The sound goes softer, now
like soaked skeins of unused yarn,
    blue hills, stacks of lost letters,
a thrumming heater, a bass guitar,
    a glass of wine. If it gets any softer,
I'll go (I promise myself). But the sound
    of the rain makes a war. I'm helpless
against it. I'm like some desperate lover
    who runs the length of a state
and then when she opens the door
    eyes like a stream, answer
unmistakable. How it falls on me
    and it falls on me
like rain, then more.
    As I hold up my arms to cover me
as I cover my head in retreat
    the water gets everywhere. I run
behind the house, where her garden of phlox
    is trampled after so much rain.
Indistinguishable. The purple petals
    are lost in weeds of green. The rain
is a quarry and sinking. The rain
    is a bathtub alone in a room.
It sounds like consequence.
    It ends like steam.

What I first said was not enough.
(One) Mounds of sawdust crowd the barn's
wooden floor, and then the bronze
    of the leftover penny. The disc's
dull shine as though slipping. The form is
    wrong. Matter misplaced. I'm
wrong. I'm kicking away the dust
    to study the floor, peeling back the rind because
underneath—a light bulb wrapped
    in string, the fruit.
If my vision had a life, it would go down
    in the planks. If I gave you the clearing
would you also dream? Little gnat that wakes me,
    the torch keeps refusing the flame. Little gnat.
Sweet lilac. (Two) The ferns finally
    unfurled. Lush, nonplussed, in clusters and blown
by an otherworldly wind. Does this convince you?
    Like kelp, they blow. Like swollen hands.
And if the brush is wet from rain
    we may not see. (Three) The Georgia quarter
dropped by the child into the communion plate. Listen.
    E Pluribus Unum. Listen. Kyrie,
Kyrie. And the church in the city,
    even the steeple fits. Let us walk home
through the squares. Let us be cogs
    with the street. I dreamt of a ruler.
And it did not move. And the cogs fit deep
    into themselves. (Four) At the edge of the turquoise
sea, a cliff; at the top of the cliff a village and
    the gardens swerve down with the hill. At the top of the village
look in the house. I'm not convinced.
    Like the well-timed click of the train leaving town
two children are moving their checkers. Black

and white; stone and stone. The thunder chokes,
sputters on. Cold in black. Blur in bright. If you look
    out the window—the water is gray
and it churls and it is the stitching
    that does not go on. You wanted to see.
I never asked you to. (Five) And we couldn't necessarily
    speak. *My heart aches.* I want to go on. Fast
world, the fitting isn't right. Whether the green
    meadow (six) on a gentle slope or (seven)
the moon framed by (eight) bright city lights, I am
    the child, swinging her feet from the bench. Look
at me with the tears cutting lines (nine)
    on my face. I'm almost opened. And
the color is about to come out.

THE CONTEMPORARY POETRY SERIES
Edited by Paul Zimmer

Dannie Abse, *One-Legged on Ice*
Susan Astor, *Dame*
Gerald Barrax, *An Audience of One*
Tony Connor, *New and Selected Poems*
Franz Douskey, *Rowing Across the Dark*
Lynn Emanuel, *Hotel Fiesta*
John Engels, *Vivaldi in Early Fall*
John Engels, *Weather-Fear: New and Selected Poems, 1958-1982*
Brendan Galvin, *Atlantic Flyway*
Brendan Galvin, *Winter Oysters*
Michael Heffernan, *The Cry of Oliver Hardy*
Michael Heffernan, *To the Wreakers of Havoc*
Conrad Hilberry, *The Moon Seen as a Slice of Pineapple*
X. J. Kennedy, *Cross Ties*
Caroline Knox, *The House Party*
Gary Margolis, *The Day We Still Stand Here*
Michael Pettit, *American Light*
Bin Ramke, *White Monkeys*
J. W. Rivers, *Proud and on My Feet*
Laurie Sheck, *Amaranth*
Myra Sklarew, *The Science of Goodbyes*
Marcia Southwick, *The Night Won't Save Anyone*
Mary Swander, *Succession*
Bruce Weigl, *The Monkey Wars*
Paul Zarzyski, *The Make-Up of Ice*

THE CONTEMPORARY POETRY SERIES
Edited by Bin Ramke

Mary Jo Bang, *The Downstream Extremity of the Isle of Swans*
J. T. Barbarese, *New Science*
J. T. Barbarese, *Under the Blue Moon*
Cal Bedient, *The Violence of the Morning*
Stephanie Brown, *Allegory of the Supermarket*
Oni Buchanan, *What Animal*
Scott Cairns, *Figures for the Ghost*
Scott Cairns, *The Translation of Babel*
Richard Chess, *Tekiah*
Richard Cole, *The Glass Children*
Martha Collins, *A History of a Small Life on a Windy Planet*
Martin Corless-Smith, *Of Piscator*
Christopher Davis, *The Patriot*
Juan Delgado, *Green Web*
Wayne Dodd, *Echoes of the Unspoken*
Wayne Dodd, *Sometimes Music Rises*
Joseph Duemer, *Customs*
Candice Favilla, *Cups*
Casey Finch, *Harming Others*
Norman Finkelstein, *Restless Messengers*
Dennis Finnell, *Belovèd Beast*
Dennis Finnell, *The Gauguin Answer Sheet*
Karen Fish, *The Cedar Canoe*
Albert Goldbarth, *Heaven and Earth: A Cosmology*
Pamela Gross, *Birds of the Night Sky/Stars of the Field*
Kathleen Halme, *Every Substance Clothed*
Jonathan Holden, *American Gothic*
Paul Hoover, *Viridian*
Tung-Hui Hu, *The Book of Motion*
Austin Hummell, *The Fugitive Kind*
Claudia Keelan, *The Secularist*
Sally Keith, *Dwelling Song*
Maurice Kilwein Guevara, *Postmortem*
Joanna Klink, *They Are Sleeping*
Caroline Knox, *To Newfoundland*
Steve Kronen, *Empirical Evidence*

Patrick Lawler, *A Drowning Man Is Never Tall Enough*

Sydney Lea, *No Sign*

Jeanne Lebow, *The Outlaw James Copeland and the Champion-Belted Empress*

Phillis Levin, *Temples and Fields*

Timothy Liu, *Of Thee I Sing*

Rachel Loden, *Hotel Imperium*

Gary Margolis, *Falling Awake*

Tod Marshall, *Dare Say*

Joshua McKinney, *Saunter*

Mark McMorris, *The Black Reeds*

Mark McMorris, *The Blaze of the Poui*

Laura Mullen, *After I Was Dead*

Jacqueline Osherow, *Conversations with Survivors*

Jacqueline Osherow, *Looking for Angels in New York*

Tracy Philpot, *Incorrect Distances*

Paisley Rekdal, *A Crash of Rhinos*

Donald Revell, *The Gaza of Winter*

Andy Robbins, *The Very Thought of You*

Martha Ronk, *Desire in L.A.*

Martha Ronk, *Eyetrouble*

Tessa Rumsey, *Assembling the Shepherd*

Peter Sacks, *O Wheel*

Aleda Shirley, *Chinese Architecture*

Pamela Stewart, *The Red Window*

Susan Stewart, *The Hive*

Donna Stonecipher, *The Reservoir*

Terese Svoboda, *All Aberration*

Terese Svoboda, *Mere Mortals*

Sam Truitt, *Vertical Elegies 5: The Section*

Lee Upton, *Approximate Darling*

Lee Upton, *Civilian Histories*

Arthur Vogelsang, *Twentieth Century Women*

Sidney Wade, *Empty Sleeves*

Liz Waldner, *Dark Would (The Missing Person)*

Marjorie Welish, *Casting Sequences*

Susan Wheeler, *Bag 'o' Diamonds*

C. D. Wright, *String Light*

Katayoon Zandvakili, *Deer Table Legs*

Andrew Zawacki, *By Reason of Breakings*